Nikos Karagiannis

History of World War
3

In June of 2016 world war 3 will end.

I will explain how this war started and how it evolved because many of these secrets are hidden from the public eye.

In 2013 Israel bombed Iran,Syria,Lebanon,Jordan,Saudi

Arabia,Egypt with nuclear missiles.They targeted the military areas sof these nations .They also bombed with nuclear,Ethiopia,Somalia,Sudan,Egypt,Yemen,Oman and United Arab Emirates with total casualties of 30 millions people.

Then Greece bombed
Israel and the hidden
Israel in southern
Turkey from the
military base of Suda
with Stealth B2
bombers.Total
casualties 15 millions
people.

Then Turkey bombed Georgia and Armenia with nuclear missiles with 4 millions dead peoples.

China bombed the state of Virginia the headquarters of the CIA with nuclear intercontintental missiles with 50 millions casualties.These casualties are the American army and the CIA.

Russia and China win the war until now.

In Ukraine a civil war started.

India started a war with nuclear warheads with China

with 100 millions
people.

The triangle of superpowers are the 3 western European nations of UK,France and Germany.They are the leaders of the planet.

The periphery of this triangle are Spain,Italy and Greece.

They are customer nations of the western European triangle. This tringle should prevail in any conflict and shoul be considered the head of earth.

States that are used for proxy wars,are Poland ,Baltic states,Ukraine and Turkey

The enemies of this triangle is Russia and China.

The triangle will allways fight wars against the nations I just mentioned.

This happens until now.

From now on I will explain my ideas how

world war 3 should
continue.

America must bomb
Nigeria and invade

Nigeria to take the oil fields of Nigeria.

They have to eliminate the Islamic terrorist threat.

The rest of the nations that I didn't mention are colonies of UK and France.

Now India must bomb Russia wil nuclear warheads and they have this capability to eliminate the Russian threat.

Ukrainians and Turks must invade Russia.

USA is a proxy war state of the western European triangle of global superpowers.

Greece must start a war against Albanians and Russians inside Greece.

Greece can bomb Albania and the Former Yugoslavia with B2 stealth bombers.

Greece has to invade Egypt and bomb Egypt.

The divide and conquer tactic that I personally use to start a war and I used to start World War 3,is very simple.

I sacrifice soldiers
from both nations ,I
blame I someone else
and I start a fight.Then
a vendetta and a war
starts between the
two nations.

The triangle of European superpower and America must fight a global war against enemies,Russia and China and I support the case of a genocide of these two nations.

When World War 3 ends in 2 years ,the triangle and USA will be the winners.

The next war ,World war 4, will have the purpose to eliminate the inferior races such as Africans

,Asians,Aboriginals ,and Indians.

The superpowers must start a global genocide against these animals.

www.ingramcontent.com/pod-product-compliance
Lightning Source LLC
Chambersburg PA
CBHW070256290526
45789CB00004B/1875